ADDER, BLUEBELL, LOBSTER

For Warren, Esther, Sam, Liv and little Sia,
with love

Text copyright © Chrissie Gittins 2016 except for
Hamster copyright © 2002, *Heron* copyright © 2010, *Otter* copyright © 2006
Illustrations copyright © Paul Bommer 2016
The right of Chrissie Gittins and Paul Bommer to be identified as the author
and illustrator of this work has been asserted by them in accordance with
the Copyright, Designs and Patents Act, 1988 (United Kingdom).

First published in Great Britain and in the USA in 2016 by
Otter-Barry Books, Little Orchard, Burley Gate, Hereford, HR1 3QS
www.otterbarrybooks.com

A catalogue record for this book is available from the British Library.

ISBN 978-1-91095-955-8

Printed in Great Britain

1 3 5 7 9 8 6 4 2

MIX
Paper from
responsible sources
FSC® C013254

ADDER, BLUEBELL, LOBSTER

Wild poems by
Chrissie Gittins

Illustrated by
Paul Bommer

Otter-Barry BOOKS

Contents

Introduction

What do these words have in common – *blackberry, hamster, leek* and *lark?* They are all words which have been deleted from the Oxford Junior Dictionary.

In 2008 Lisa Saunders was helping her son with his homework in Northern Ireland. She discovered that *moss* and *fern* were missing from her copy of the dictionary. Dictionary makers don't tell us what they take out of their books, so Lisa painstakingly compared six editions dating from 1978 to 2007. She discovered that over 100 words had been withdrawn – words which name animals, birds, pets, fish and nuts; words which name trees, fruits, reptiles, vegetables, fungi, flowers and plants.

You will no longer find *buttercup*, *goldfish* or *wren* in its pages, or *leopard*, *almond* or *primrose*. And if you want to think and write about gorse flooding the hillsides with yellow each spring, or spinach getting stuck in your teeth, you won't find the definition or spelling of *gorse* or *spinach*.

The words that were taken out of the dictionary have been replaced by technological words – *blog, broadband, cut and paste* – and words such as *celebrity, vandalism* and *negotiate*. These are all useful words and I wouldn't want to argue that one set of words is more necessary than another, but I'm sad that the words about nature have been elbowed out.

The natural world is just as vital as it ever was. We see the seasons change, hear birds sing and grow vegetables in the countryside *and* in the city. How wonderful to find a sea of bluebells in a quiet wood, or to see the sun silver the underside of willow leaves as the wind flips them up beside an urban river.

I wanted to recapture some of these words and to help restore their value, so I have chosen 40 as titles for the poems in this book. There are another 70 words which have been deleted, which I haven't yet written poems about. So if you'd like to see the whole list, go to the Campaigns page at www.naturemusicpoetry.com

Perhaps you'd like to write some of your own poems. It might be a good excuse for an adventure! I had great fun exploring Quarry Wood in Kent for bluebells, watching a heron on the lake at Crystal Palace Park, and studying the lobster in the Horniman Museum Aquarium. I strolled along the Ravensbourne River in Lewisham looking at the willows, and I discovered an otter in the River Torridge in Devon.

Have fun exploring, and I really hope you enjoy these poems.

Chrissie Gittins

Adder

If you add an adder to an adder
        they are prone to have a dance,
                they writhe around each other
                        till the strongest gets a chance
                to PUSH the other down.

Belly to belly or back to back
        they prance along the ground,
                the winner wins the lady snake
        and so romance begins.

He flicks his tongue along her sides
        and down her zig zag back,
                three months on the babes are born –
    tiny snakes in miniature, protected in a sac.

So if you see an adder, basking in the midday sun,
        remember they are timid,
                    there is no need to run –
        they only use their venom
if caught, or trodden on!

Allotment

When it rains the soil sighs deeply,

the leaves of the purple sprouting broccoli giggle as the rivulets tickle their veins,

rainbow chard reaches out to catch droplets in its wrinkles,

the strawberries smile – their redness becomes redder, their sweetness sweeter,

broad beans swell inside their emerald pods

waiting to be picked.

Rain trickles over tiny shiny apples,

it surprises the purple bean flowers as it slips between their petals,

it sinks beneath the leeks, making them strong and white for a winter feast.

When the sun appears the soil sighs again,

and everything grows three inches taller!

13

Beetroot

The beetroot is a bossy veg,
inside it's deep maroon,

it comes into your kitchen
and paints the entire room.

The juice gets on your fingers,
the juice gets on the walls,

when you rinse your fingers –
a red Niagara Falls!

The beet leaps on the oven
and tells you what to do –

"Bake me, boil me, grate me,
slice me with a knife,

whizz me into tasty soup
but don't go through your life

without my redness on your tongue;
enjoy my velvet texture –

then sing this Beetroot Song!"

Bluebell

April forest friend through May
they shimmer three feet above the ground –

a cobalt belt, a lake of bell towers
nodding onwards in the wind.

Lance leaves, buds hugging up the stem –
they drop, open, petals peeling back

to witches' thimbles, free then to ring
their bells at midnight.

Beware a starry walk,
for if you hear this tintinnabulation

you may find your breath too short and sharp to wake.
Best walk in dappled shade,

step gingerly between each bulb,
relish their constancy,

their bank on bank of vertiginous blue light.

Blackberry

luscious globules
purple dribbles
apple's friend
crumble filling

thorny picking
bluey fingers
pimple curer
winter jam

brambleberries
brumblekites
bramble ramble
pie delights

Catkin

Snow falls on branches
buds of sleeping silver fur
the promise of jade

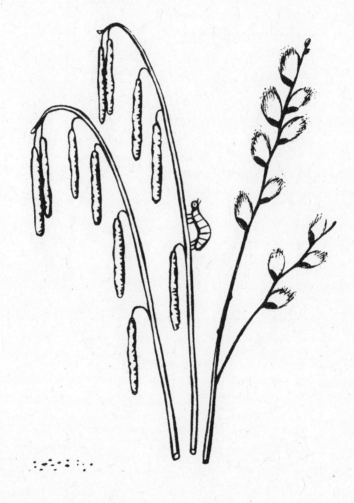

Cauliflower

Never take flour in the shower,
take a firm white cauliflower.

It's always pleasant to have an hour
in the shower

with a globular cauliflower –
especially if the shower

is a power shower.

Cheetah

You may envy my speed –
      fastest animal on the land, no need to cheat.
You may envy my acceleration –
      from zero to forty miles an hour, in three strides.
You may envy my extra-long eyes –
        giving me wide-angle views of the savannah
      at seventy-five miles an hour.

I sit, poised on a termite mound,
                scanning the horizon for prey –
gazelle, warthog, rabbit.

But my weakness is in my strength.
      After the chase my oversized heart needs rest;
            hot and winded I must wait to eat,
keeping a lookout – lion, leopard, hyena.
      My slender head, short muzzle,
          help me slip through the air;
but my jaw is weak, my teeth are small.
      I am no match when I become the prey –
I run, I don't fight.

                  I'm made for flight.

Conker

I hang, lime green, from a sturdy tree,
encased in a spiky shell,
like a rolled-up baby hedgehog.

Inside I'm rich brown, shiny,
like the toes of shoes
brushed with dark tan polish.

A white scar spreads across me
like the surface of the moon.

Boil me in vinegar if you want
to make me even harder,
drill me through,
thread me with string,
tie a thick securing knot.

Now I'm a *none-er,*
I may become a *two-er,*
or even a *three-er.*

Thwack me against your friends' conkers,
swing and hit and hit and hit and hit till I split.

Then find another.

Dandelion

I have a clock which doesn't tick,
I have a clock which doesn't tock.
I have a head which doesn't see,
I have a head which says 'Blow me'!

My flower is like the sun,
my clock is like the moon,
my seeds are tiny stars
which will be flowers very soon.

My name means *teeth of lion*,
it describes my toothy greens
which you can eat in salads and sandwiches –
food fit for famished queens.

The word *dandelion* comes from the French *dent de lion* – teeth of lion.

F

Fern

What I love about ferns are their fronds.

What I love about ferns are their shapes.

What I love about ferns are the way their new fronds curl up tightly.

What I love about ferns are the way their fronds unfurl.

What I love about ferns is that they can live for 100 years.

What I love about ferns is that they've been on this planet for 360 million years.

What I love about ferns is that they can live together in a fernery.

What I love about ferns is the way they stroke the trunks of trees on the forest floor.

What I love about ferns is that they can clean polluted air.

What I love about ferns is their names –
common staghorn fern, bird's nest fern,
hart's-tongue fern, liquorice fern,
ostrich fern, interrupted fern.

Fungi
Chanterelle

Mademoiselle Chanterelle –
how did you become so yellow?

I drank a cup of golden sun
just as the day was done.

Mademoiselle Chanterelle –
why do you smell of apricot?

I inhaled the perfume
when it passed by on a zephyr.

Mademoiselle Chanterelle –
why do you taste so peppery?

I fear my temper is quick and sharp,
my flesh is fiery too.

Mademoiselle Chanterelle –
Will you come and simmer in my cooking pot?

You'll have to find me first!

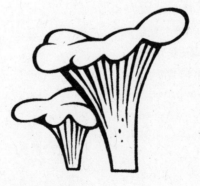

Giant Puffball
(Calvatia Gigantea)

I'm outraged by the meaning of my Latin name!
It could've been –
'a white almost globe',
'a ball of thick cream cheese',
'a sphere of matt kid leather',
'holder of a trillion spores'.
Instead it's 'giant bald head'!
I'm so much more.

You can come across me in
meadows, fields and forests,
glowing in the undergrowth
until the raindrops fall
and I spew forth my brown spores
in a puff of fine powder
to make many many more
'succulent velvet wondrous orbs'.

Gorse

I blaze across the countryside
on moors and heaths close by the sea,
my golden flowers erupt,
but first you might smell me.

Coconut and vanilla
carrying on the breeze,
you may also hear popping,
and the sound of clouds of bees.

The popping is my seedheads,
they dry out in the heat,
then crack and twist and flick the seed
as far as thirty feet.

Remember if you hear that when I'm out of bloom
kissing's out of fashion,
that in fact my lemon flowers
always always blossom!

Gorse is also known as *furze* and *whin*.

Hamster

Harry the hamster, in his ball,
rolled round the bedroom,
rolled round the hall.
He rolled to the bathroom,
he rolled to the stairs
where a huge teddy bear
took him clean unawares.

He rolled slap-bang into
the honey hall wall,
but that didn't stop him,
for he was so small
and a whole world awaited
Harry in his ball.

On Monday he rolled down the garden,
on Tuesday he rolled down the road,
on Thursday he rolled down a bike path
till he was stopped in his tracks by a toad.

On Friday he rolled to New Brighton,
on Saturday to warm Singapore,
on Sunday he yawned, climbed back
in his cage, and all day
simply rolled in his straw.

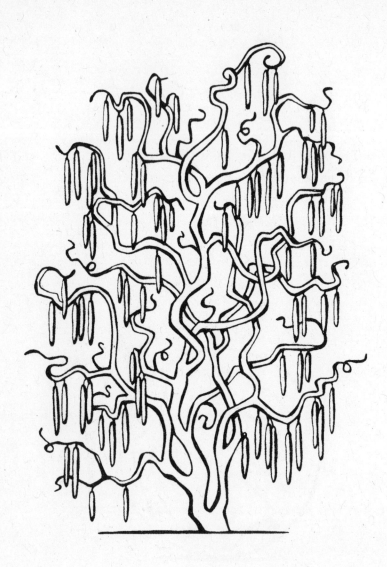

Hazel

I'm a street-dance tree,
I bend and I curl,
my branches are contorted,
I curve and I whirl.

I'm a corkscrew hazel,
my twigs spiral and whirl,
I have golden yellow catkins,
I twist and I twirl.

I'm a Hazel Contorta,
each arm a curlicue,
best seen in winter
against a sky of powder blue.

Heron

Broken black streaks
feather his throat,

black eyebrows shoot
into a Mandarin's moustache.

Eyes staring ahead,
rigid as the cement pterodactyl

in flight to his right,
head darts down.

He straightens with a fish in his beak,
slowly gulping,

like sucking
on a saved caramel.

Ivy

Berries in winter
leaf litter warms woodland floor
creatures snuffle through

Lark

You'll hear me before you see me,
spilling notes from high skies,
I don't pause for breath –
my song, without doubt, is the best.

You might see me as a speck in the clouds,
I'll grow bigger, disappear altogether,
but still I'm thrilling the heavens,
hanging over the land.

I dare any another lark to come near,
I'll thrash him out of my patch
filling the atmosphere with
my thirty-six notes a second.

I'm second to none,
dive-bombing back through the sky
to keep a fair eye on my mate
as she waits in the grass.

We have wide-mouthed babies to make.

Lavender

Lie in your bath and inhale the exquisite scent.

Avoid flies and mosquitoes with a dab of oil to your wrists, neck and ankles.

Very useful for teachers in Provence who crush the seeds to calm their class.

Egyptians, when mummified, were wrapped in lavender-dipped clothes.

Not only blue, purple, pink, white and yellow flowers – but green ones too!

Do you know you can use it to sooth aching muscles, headaches, burns, motion sickness and nightmares?

Even used on the battlefields of World Wars One and Two to prevent infection and relieve pain.

Recipes with lavender include shortbread, scones, ice cream, lemonade and roast potatoes!

Leek

Leeks like a cheese sauce,
Leeks like a tart,
Leeks can be a main course,
Leeks can be a start.

Leeks can be roasted,
Leeks can be steamed,
Leeks can be microwaved,
And leeks can be creamed.

Leeks are part of the lily family –
Tender, mild and sweet.
They help stave off winter colds
And are divine to eat.

Put them with potato
In soup on a snowy day,
To warm up your tummy
Before you go out and play.

Lobster

For the Horniman Museum Aquarium lobster.
(He didn't move an inch from behind a rock
when I went to see him.)

If you see me in a murky situation,
if I appear lazy, and lacking motivation,
you may draw the clear conclusion
that I'm suffering the crustacean blues.

If I'm still, and have no conversation,
if I seem lost in endless meditation,
if my claws flap up in irritation,
it'll be those darn crustacean blues.

If I will eat neither mollusc nor vegetation,
if I have no interest in mild flirtation,
if I seem to abandon my education,
you can bet I have those tough crustacean blues.

But when I start to think of my vacation,
my antennae circle in anticipation,
when I know that Cornwall is my destination,
you can be sure I'm cured of those crustacean blues.

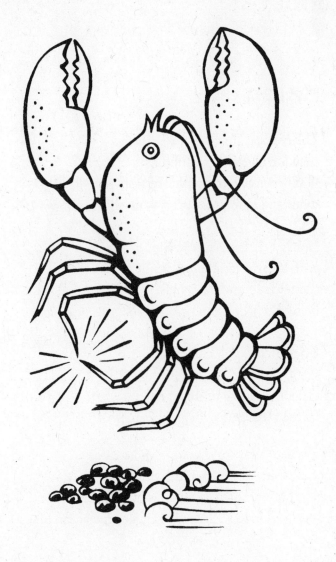

Melon

The melons are having a party,
they are all rolling around,
Watermelon is red with exertion,
when they jump, there's a squelching sound.

Honeydew is wearing yellow
with a sharp lime-green inside,
Cantaloupe prefers orange,
he wears his mottled green coat with pride.

Frogskin is going bananas,
she's leaping right into the air,
Galia is running with juice,
taking it easy in a cucumber chair.

Cucumbers are cousins of melons,
squashes are close relatives too,
and when the party is over
they all form an orderly queue.

Frogskin rolls behind Galia,
Cantaloupe brings up the rear,
Honeydew holds hands with Watermelon –
they can't wait for their party next year!

Mint

You can eat mint sauce with a slice of roast lamb
But you can't clean your teeth with it.

You can brush your teeth with minty toothpaste
But you can't make it into ice cream.

You can eat a cornet of chocolate mint ice cream
But it won't keep the bugs at bay.

A pot of mint will keep flies and ants away
But you will need boiling water to make it into tea.

You can drink a mug of peppermint tea
But you can't drink peppermint creams.

You can eat a box of peppermint creams
But you have to climb a mountain to eat
    Kendal Mint Cake.

Kendal Mint Cake will give you energy
        at the top of a mountain
But you can't eat after dinner mints until
        you've eaten your dinner.

Your dinner is a thick slice of roast lamb
With a slurp of fresh mint sauce.

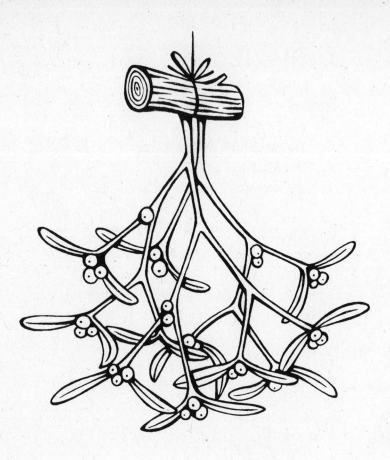

58

Mistletoe

Mistletoe, mistletoe,
I see you high up in the tree,
a tangled ball of leaves,
a windy place to be.

Mistletoe, mistletoe,
growing on the tree,
drinking from its branches,
giving pollen to a bee.

Mistletoe, mistletoe,
your berries are like pearls,
they glow in winter darkness,
until the spring unfurls.

Mistletoe, mistletoe,
a place for birds to nest,
a wish for peace in the New Year,
for friendship East and West.

Newt

I'm a cute, cute newt.
I have warts and spots and I'm cute.
I'm slimy and jagged,
I can poison my foes
and I'm cute.

I can grow lost limbs,
I have a blotchy orange belly,
my tail lashes out
and I'm cute.

I'm a cold-blooded creature
with a price on my head,
I eat slugs from your garden,
gobs of frogspawn from your pond.
I eat snails and worms and spiders
and bees and mosquitoes and ants,
but most of all
I'M
CUTE!

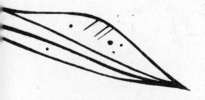

Great Crested Newts are protected and there is a £5,000 ($7,500) fine for harming them.

Otter

I knew the river hid
behind the bank,
lying, like a length of silk,
stretched between the willows.

The surface ripped,
something dived –
gone too long to be a bird.

Eager head above the water,
down he went again,
a flash of oily fur.

He swam up beside,
this time he stayed,
looking at me straight.
I walked to keep his pace.

I loved his length –
his tail his body,
his body his tail,
his tail the river's length.

We moved together
through the wind,
along the river's course.

Another dive,
I skimmed the current,
searching for his guise.

He'd gone on alone.
I felt him though,
gliding through
the river's strength.

Parsnip

Twinkle, twinkle, little parsnip,
How I wonder what you are!
In the spring we plant your seeds,
Underground your roots grow far.
Twinkle, twinkle, little parsnip,
Growing beneath the bright North Star.

Twinkle, twinkle, little parsnip,
How I wonder at your hardship.
For it's when the biting frost is here
That your sweet flavour becomes clear.
Twinkle, twinkle, little parsnip,
I like to eat you with honey and garlic!

Pelican

There's a photo in our family album
of me at Chester Zoo.
I'm holding up a slice of bread
too high for the pelican to peck.

Dad took too long to take the shot,
the pelican got impatient.
He opened up his massive beak,
and locked both sides around my neck!

Plaice

I lie like a brown plate on the sea floor,
my orange spots covered in sand,
my white underside resting on grit.
I can stay like this for hours,
keeping my secret.

If a clam comes along
I might vacuum him up,
crushing the shell with my long jaws.

Occasionally I glide out,
fluttering my fins,
being careful to swim round fishing lines.
I'm not fooled by their sequins and beads –
no easy catch.

You might think I look grumpy
with my upside-down smile, but no –
I'm thinking of my secret.

How when I was tiny,
just hatched from my egg,
I had one eye on my upper side
and one eye underneath.

Gradually, my eye below
moved round to join my other eye.
It's way more comfortable,
and it makes me a much better spy.

Poppy

Choose a sunny patch of soil,
take a moment to look up at the clear blue sky,
rake the ground, remove weeds and any large stones,
look out for the robin who likes to keep you company.
Sow between March and May when the soil is warm.
You'll find my seeds are the tiniest so careful not to
drop me; make narrow channels in the soil,
scatter me thinly along the rows.
Water regularly to encourage
me to grow.

When my seedlings are
large enough to hold, thin out so
we have enough room. My petals will be
the thinnest, paperiest petals you've ever seen.
My flowers will last a matter of days, but their redness
will stay in your mind through winter. When my flowers
die there will be seed pods like pepper pots. Let them dry,
turn them upside down and shake them into
a paper bag. Next year, choose a sunny patch
of soil, remember to look at the sky,
look out for the robin, rake
the rich dark ground.

Porcupine

I'm a punk and I'm a porcupine,
my spines are brown and white,
I can balance well on branches
and I can try with all my might
to jump between two trees –
but really I just can't.

I must slither down the tree trunk
and walk along the ground,
then climb up the next tree
with a scurry scrunchy sound.

If a leopard comes towards me
my quills stand up straight.
I show him my rear end
and jab with all my weight
till the quills lodge deep
in his legs and face and neck.

My spikes soon replace themselves
so I'm ready for the next.
I like to leave lions, especially,
well and truly vexed.

Raven

If you see a black bird rolling down a slope in the snow –
it's a raven.

If you see a black bird sliding down a snowy roof –
it's a raven.

If you hear a black bird imitating a toilet flush –
it's a raven.

If you see a black bird playing with sticks, pine cones
    or golf balls –
it's a raven.

If you see a black bird in the sky with a diamond-shaped
    tail –
it's a raven.

If you see a black bird making fun of other creatures –
it's a raven.

If you see a black bird pulling a fisherman's line out of
    an ice hole to steal his fish –
it's a raven.

If you see a black bird pointing with its beak –
it's a raven.

If you see a black bird comforting another black bird
    after it's lost a fight –
it's a raven.

If you see a black bird pushing a rock on a man to stop
    him climbing to its nest –
it's a raven.

If you see a black bird celebrating its 30th birthday –
it's a raven.

If you hear a flock of crows laughing madly –
they are ravens.

If you see a black bird standing on the lawn for an hour
    sunbathing –
it's a blackbird!

Rhubarb

I am a stick of rhubarb,
I grew up in a shed,
they forced me in the darkness
until my stem was red.

The shed was warm and sprayed with rain,
I dreamt each night of light,
day by day I grew an inch,
I stretched with all my might.

You could hear our leaf buds popping,
the creaking of our stems
as we reached towards the ceiling
till our leaves had yellow ends.

We were harvested by candlelight
and laid out in a truck,
we zoomed along the motorway
and arrived at four o'clock.

I finished up in Pimlico
on a greengrocer's shop display,
a lady bought me for her tea –
I discovered to my dismay

that I would become a crumble
piled high with sugar and flour,
swallowed in an instant, on a cold May day,
as her children cried, "More, more, more!"

Starling

starlings swirl
  starlings chuckle
starlings bicker
and starlings d
                a
                  z
                    zle

                    starlings click
                        starlings trill
                            starlings soar
                    and starlings r
                              a
                                z
                                  z
                                    le

                        starlings whirr
                    starlings bustle
            starlings flock
and starlings sh
            uff
              le

            starlings hurry
                starlings scream

78

                    starlings whoosh
and starlings s
                qua
                  b
                  ble

starlings swoop
     starlings chatter
starlings swarm
and they
        cloud the sky with the most
                        amazing
                                murmurations

Stoat

My favourite food is rabbit,
if chasing doesn't work,
I call upon my superpower
and make my body jerk.

I flip and roll and spin,
jumping high up in the air,
the rabbit sees me whizzing round
and all he does is stare.

I dash and twist and tumble,
inching closer to my prey,
the rabbit sits, hypnotised –
he won't see another day.

I jump aboard his back,
sink my teeth into his neck,
he flops over on the ground,
I can hear his soft bones crack.

I drag him to my burrow,
you see it really isn't wise
to be taken in by my antics –
I kill rabbits ten times my size.

Tulip

First there is a nugget bulb,
shiny, with papery case.

Then a pointed emerald shoot
pushes through frozen soil.

It points its hands to show us leaves,
then stretches up to hold a bud.

The petals, sleek, spread more each day,
splashing pink or white or red –

their swirling skirts want their own way,
they wave and throw their arms about.

Careless of their bending stems
the tulips dance in hail and rain.

Petals droop, and drop and dry –
we hope the bulb will bloom again.

Violet

Vio-vio-violet how did you get so delicate?
Vio-vio-violet why are you so blue?

Vio-vio-violet who made your leaves in heart shapes?
And who painted veins all over you?

My leaves are for your tenderness,
My veins are constant through and through.

A violet is violet,
I speak of spring to you.

Willow

I am a willow in the middle of a plate,
    I lean towards the water, as willows do.
                My bark is clawed with striations,
    my leaves flip up, blinking silver.

Two lovers canoodled beneath my branches –
    Koong-se, the daughter of a grand Mandarin,
           and Chang, the Mandarin's secretary,
                who had no money to his name.

When the Mandarin discovered their love
        his tiered pagoda shook with rage.
                First he banished Chang,
    then he built a high fence around his grounds.
Each day Koong-se wailed beneath my branches.

Until one dark wet Tuesday she saw
      a shell boat floating towards her.
        In it was a bead she'd given to Chang,
          so she knew that he must be safe and near.

Meanwhile the Mandarin had found
a noble Duke to marry his mournful daughter.
He sailed towards the pagoda with a cascade
of priceless jewels in a golden casket.
Koong-se's heart sank like a huge boulder
thrown into the cold river.

Chang dressed as a servant
and slipped behind the Mandarin and the Duke
as they lay slumped over their feasting table,
brim full of wine.

Chang found Koon-se in her room,
they held onto each other like the roots of a tree
clinging to a falling cliff.
Slowly they crept downstairs.
All the guests and servants were sleeping,
but just as they escaped through the door
the Mandarin stirred and opened one bloodshot eye.

He stood and shouted and bawled
and chased them over the bridge.
They ran straight past me –
Koong-se's red silk kimono caught on my rough bark.

Chang and Koong-se escaped to a distant land.
Chang wrote stories of fiery dragons and terrifying tigers.
His fame spread far –
so far that the Mandarin heard all about him.

He sent his guards to seek them out.
Chang was slain quickly with a bronze sword.
Koong-se knew she couldn't live a day without him.
She set fire to her house and stood
looking at the mountains as
the flames flickered around her.

At that very moment the gods turned them into
two white doves for all eternity.
They fly together to this day –
dipping and hovering and swirling

through the deafening skies.

Wren

I have places to go
and places to be,
I'm hopping and dashing –
you'll never catch me.

A seed here and a spider there,
I'm peering and rooting –
I've mouths to feed.

My mate built me eleven nests,
I had to choose which one I liked best.

When it's cold and wintry and snow's ahead
we do the sensible thing –
sleep ten to a bed!

Acknowledgements

'Hamster' was first published in *Now You See Me, Now You ...* (Rabbit Hole Publications, 2002)

'Otter' was first published in *I Don't Want an Avocado for an Uncle* (Rabbit Hole Publications, 2006)

'Heron' was first published in *The Humpback's Wail* (Rabbit Hole Publications, 2010)

With grateful thanks to Carol Robinson (la Botaniste Anglaise) for her natural history advice.

Paul Bommer is an artist, print-maker and illustrator, who works from his studio in Norfolk. Clients include Fortnum & Mason, Greene King, the London Guildhall, Angela Hartnett, Harrods, the Guardian and many others. He was the illustrator for *The Humpback's Wail*, by Chrissie Gittins.

You can find out more about Paul Bommer's work at **www.paulbommer.com** and paulbommer.blogspot.it

Chrissie Gittins was born in Lancashire and lives in south London. She worked as an artist and teacher before becoming a full-time writer.

She has been shortlisted twice for the CLPE Poetry Award, her poems have been animated for CBeebies and included in many anthologies. She visits schools, libraries and book festivals across the UK. She has read her poems in Shetland, West Cork, Bangkok and New York.

Chrissie won the Belmont Poetry Prize for children's poems in 2002, and her first three children's poetry collections were all Poetry Book Society Choices. Her poetry books for children are: *The Listening Station, Now You See Me, Now You...*, *I Don't Want an Avocado for an Uncle, The Humpback's Wail,* and *Stars in Jars*, which was a Scottish Poetry Library recommendation for 2014.

Chrissie was a finalist in the first Manchester Children's Literature Prize in 2014 with a portfolio of new poems. She is featured on the Poetry Archive, and you can find out more about her work on her website: www.chrissiegittins.co.uk